Godmersham Park
Kent

Jane Austen*

Edward

Elizabeth

* By courtesy of the National Portrait Gallery

Godmersham Park, Kent

**before, during and since
Jane Austen's day**

NIGEL NICOLSON

The Jane Austen Society

First published in Great Britain 1996
by The Jane Austen Society
Carton House, Medstead,
Alton, Hampshire

ISBN 0 9511035 6 3

A catalogue record for this book is available from the British Library

Printed in Great Britain by Sarsen Press, 22 Hyde Street, Winchester SO23 7DR

Introduction

The discovery of a handwritten illustrated catalogue advertising the sale of Godmersham in 1874 by Edward Knight (1794-1879), the elder son of Edward Knight (Austen), led to the publication of this booklet. The catalogue had been found at Chawton House in Hampshire by Richard Knight, a direct descendant of Edward Knight and President of the Jane Austen Society.

The catalogue, which included a plan of the interior of the house, demonstrated the many changes that had been made since the sale in 1874. Nigel Nicolson, who has already written extensively on houses in Kent, kindly agreed to write an article about the various architectural changes to the house before and after 1874. His extensive research transformed the proposed article into this booklet.

Our thanks are due to Nigel Nicolson for this delightful and fascinating study, and to John Sunley, the present owner of Godmersham, for generously supporting the production of this publication.

It is hoped that the detailed information presented here will be of considerable interest not only to Jane Austen's admirers but also to those living in the county of Kent and beyond its borders.

ALWYN AUSTEN

IT IS WELL KNOWN that Jane Austen's elder brother Edward was adopted as a boy by his father's distant cousin, Thomas Knight, the owner of Godmersham Park, a beautiful eighteenth-century house which lies in the valley of the River Stour between Ashford and Canterbury. Thomas made Edward his heir, but on Thomas's death in 1794 his widow inherited his estates for her lifetime, with reversion to Edward when she died. However, in 1797 she decided to anticipate the bequest and she persuaded him to move to Godmersham with his growing family while she spent her remaining years in Canterbury. In compliance with his benefactor's Will, Edward changed his name to Knight, which did not please his children, one of whom, Fanny, wrote, 'We are all therefore Knights, instead of dear old Austens! How I hate it!!!!!!'[1]

Nevertheless, Godmersham came as a great boon to the whole Austen family. Edward was lavish with hospitality to his siblings. Jane and her sister Cassandra were frequent visitors there between 1798 and 1813, and Jane wrote many of her surviving letters to and from the house when she and Cassandra were staying there separately. If we are to believe the old-age reminiscences of another of her nieces, Marianne, she continued to work on her current novel during her visits and would read aloud passages from it to the

---

[1] Margaret Wilson, *Almost Another sister* (Kent County Council 1990), p.18.

Fig. 1 *The house as it appeared from the north at the time of Jane Aus* *original 1732 house* (from Hasted's *History of Kent*, 2nd edition, 1790).

its in the 1790s. Thomas Knight's two wings had just been added to the

9

elder girls. She was probably thinking of Jane's visit in 1813, when Marianne was 12, and Jane was either making notes for *Emma* or writing a fair-copy of *Mansfield Park*.[2]

Godmersham is therefore more closely connected with Jane Austen's life and work than any other surviving house except Chawton Cottage. Her visits often lasted for months on end. Apart from the pleasure she took in the company of her brother and his family, she loved the place for its 'Elegance & Ease & Luxury', as she once wrote to Cassandra,[3] and for the variety of social life that it offered, much wider than that at Steventon, where she was born and spent the first twenty-five years of her life, and Chawton where she lived for her last and most productive years. There can be little doubt that while she was staying there she derived many ideas for her fictional characters and places from their frequent parties and expeditions. Godmersham is not 'Rosings' or 'Pemberley' or 'Sotherton', but her visits gave her an intimate acquaintance with life in a great country house and the management of a large estate.

Although the house survives in perfect condition, its garden front and the arrangement of the rooms

---

[2] See *Jane Austen: A Family Record*, revised by Deirdre Le Faye (British Library 1989), p.184.

[3] *Jane Austen's Letters*, 3rd edition, ed. Deirdre Le Faye (Oxford 1995), Letter 55.

have been greatly altered since her death, having undergone two major constructions in 1853-5 and 1935-8, and at intervals minor changes to suit the needs of successive occupants, including the present tenants, Infocheck Equifax Europe, who have transformed it into one of the most elegant offices in England.

In imagination we must peel away what has been added since Jane's death in 1817, and replace what has been subtracted, in order to recreate the house which she knew. We are assisted by four sets of documents which have not previously been consulted in this context. They are:

1   A detailed historical survey of the park by Dr. Nicola Bannister, which reproduces many contemporary maps and plans.[4]

2   The vendor's copy of the sale-catalogue of 1874, with manuscript additions, loaned by Richard Knight, President of the Jane Austen Society.

3   A set of early architectural drawings of the house preserved in the Centre for Kentish Studies in County Hall, Maidstone.

4   The 1935-8 architectural drawings which Mr Greg Ellis, estate manager of the Sunley Farms, has allowed me to examine.

---

[4] *Godmersham Park: An Historic Landscape Survey*, Nicola R. Bannister (Funded by English Heritage, 1995).

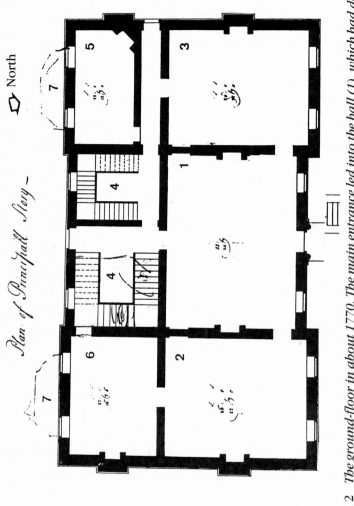

Fig. 2 *The ground-floor in about 1770. The main entrance led into the hall (1), which had doors to the drawing-room (2) and dining-room (3), and ahead to the staircases (4), one of which was abolished. In Jane Austen's day the breakfast-room was probably (5) and the south drawing-room (6). The bay windows to these two rooms (7), added in the 1780s, are lightly sketched in by a contemporary hand. The plan was made before the addition of the two wings.* (Centre for Kentish Studies, Maidstone)

In addition, I have consulted the volume on North East and East Kent by John Newman in the Nikolaus Pevsner series *The Buildings of England*, and the early Ordnance Survey maps of the district in the Map Library of the British Museum.

Godmersham was built in about 1732 by Thomas Knight, father of Edward Austen's benefactor, who changed his name twice, first to May from Brodnax (the family which had owned the manor since 1590), and then from May to Knight, each change bringing with it a substantial legacy, including the manors of Steventon and Chawton in Hampshire. Knight's architect for the new Godmersham, built on the site of the Elizabethan house, is unknown, but Christopher Hussey suggested[5] that its distinction is worthy of Roger Morris, who designed Marble Hill, Twickenham, in 1724. The plasterwork and carved wood in two of the main rooms are comparable in quality to those of Mereworth Castle, its Kentish near-contemporary. It was a brick house of two storeys, with an attic storey inset with dormer windows. From the drive one entered a superb hall, paved in black and white, from which opened a staircase hall and four main rooms, as shown on the plan (fig. 2) in the Maidstone archives. During the last years of his long life (1702-81) Thomas Knight senior added two matching wings to the

---

[5] *Country Life,* 16 February 1945.

entrance front, the eastern to contain a long library, and the western to expand the services of the house including a new kitchen. The wings were linked to the main house by low pavilions.

This was the house that his son, Thomas Knight junior, inherited in 1781, and its appearance from the north is illustrated (fig. 1) in Hasted's *History of Kent* (1790) by an engraving which only slightly pre-dates Jane Austen's first visit. She would have driven from Canterbury over the hill past Chilham Castle by a road which curved down the valley on the west side of the River Stour (it was not re-routed to the other side, the present A28, until the 1830s), and the house would have been visible across the wooded and deer-stocked park from almost a mile away, lying low between two saddles of the Downs, the northern carrying the Pilgrim's Way and the other a classical temple in the Doric style built by Thomas Knight senior in about 1770. If she had approached from the south, she would have passed the existing church,[6] a large medieval barn, a house called Godmersham Court Lodge, which stood till the 1950s, the vicarage, a school house, and a huddle of cottages between the river and the mansion (fig. 3). To the north there were two walled gardens and an orchard, sketched in the

---

[6] For alterations to the church, and the family's connections with it, see *The Church of St Laurence, Godmersham,* Tim Tatton-Brown, *Archaeologia Cantiana* CVI (1989).

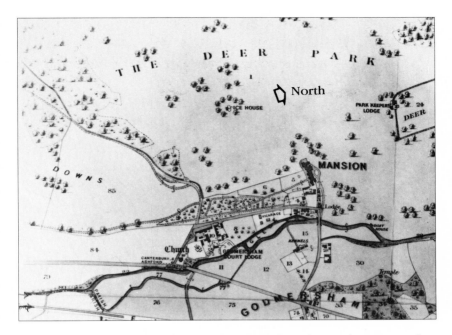

Fig. 3 *Part of the estate-map of 1874, from the sale-catalogue issued in that year. The north is to the right. The River Stour bisects the map, and above it is the main house. The church is to the left. Between them are the gardens and Bentigh through which Jane Austen walked to church.*

Andrews & Dury map of 1779 (see Bannister, *loc.cit.*). Along one side of these enclosures was an avenue of limes and yews, called Bentigh, which Jane Austen mentions in her letters more than once, and which was not destroyed until the great storm of 1987. It has since been replanted.

The entrance front is unaltered to this day, but the south or garden front is much changed and the original disposition of the rooms is not entirely clear.

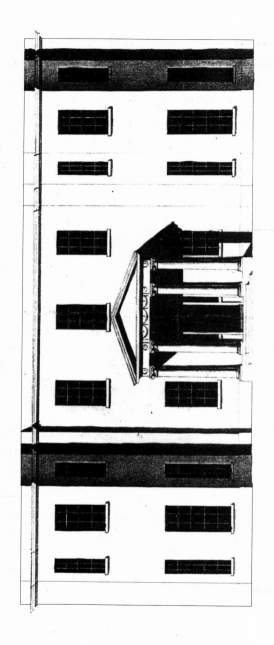

Fig. 4   An architect's drawing for the south front (omitting the roof) in about 1785, showing the two bay windows and the Ionic porch which Thomas Knight junior added to the original façade. (Centre for Kentish Studies, Maidstone)

16

Roughly pencilled on the eighteenth-century plan of the ground floor (fig. 2) are the outlines of two bay windows. These were constructed, perhaps by Thomas Knight junior in the 1780s, when he added the portico supported by four Ionic columns to give this front greater distinction. We see the result in an elevation of about 1785 in the Centre for Kentish Studies drawing (fig. 4), and these features are clearly outlined in a parish map of 1815.[7]

For the arrangement and use of the rooms we are largely dependent on matching the surviving floor plans with the letters which Jane Austen and her niece Fanny Knight wrote in the house. The interior was not unlike that of Sotherton in *Mansfield Park*:

A number of rooms, all lofty, and many large, and amply furnished in the taste of fifty years back, with shining floors, solid mahogany, rich damask, marble, gilding and carving, each handsome in its way.

Behind the entrance hall (fig. 5), the scene of many a family greeting, was the main staircase where one would expect to find a saloon. An exit to the garden lay beyond it.[8] To the left of the hall was the much-ornamented drawing room, which Jane never mentions in her letters, and to the right was the dining

---

[7] In the Public Library, Ashford. Reproduced by Bannister, *loc.cit.*

[8] Illustrated opposite p.198 of *Jane Austen: Her Homes and her Friends* by Constance Hill (1902).

Fig. 5   *The main hall in 1945 (Country Life). It was built and embellished in the 1730s, and apart from the furnishing, it remains unchanged to this day.*

18

room, from where she could watch coaches crossing the park as she sat at dinner (see Letter 52). This leaves the 'breakfast parlour', which was presumably the south-west corner-room, since Fanny mentions that her aviary stood between it and the portico,[9] and the 'south' drawing room with the other bay window. Two more living rooms were added after the eighteenth-century plan was drawn. One was the billiards room, constructed partly from the link-pavilion on the east side, and the other was the library.

The billiards-table must have been one of Edward's later additions, for in 1813 (Letter 92) Jane describes it as a new attraction for the gentlemen. But the library counted for more. It was the most important room in Jane Austen's Godmersham life, where she spent many hours 'in warm and happy solitude' (Letter 55).

In his edition of the Letters (Vol.II, note to p.368, repeated by Le Faye, p.426), R.W. Chapman identifies this library as 'probably a smaller room' on the south or garden side. For several reasons this guess must be wrong. In a contemporary description of the house,[10] a visitor speaks of 'two wings, one of which, the eastern, contains a most excellent library', and it is still so-named and located on the 1874 ground-plan (fig. 6). Jane Austen's Letters contain two further clues. She writes (Letter 89), 'I am now alone in the Library,

---

[9] Wilson, *Almost Another Sister,* p.10.

[10] *Tour through the Isle of Thanet* by Zechariah Cozens (1793).

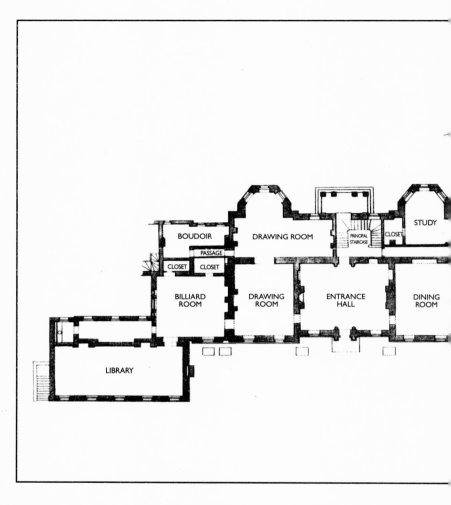

Fig. 6   *The plan of the ground-floor in 1874, from the sales-brochure of*
was the work of Edward Knight junior in the 1850s and was demolished
bottom-left. (Reproduced by permission of Richard Knight)

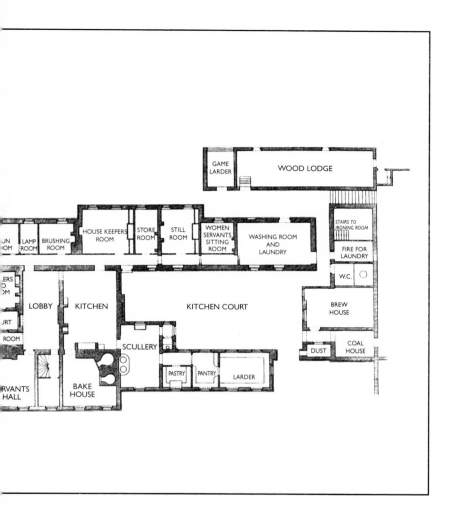

GAME
LARDER

WOOD LODGE

STAIRS TO
IRONING ROOM

FIRE FOR
LAUNDRY

HOUSE KEEPERS
ROOM

STORE
ROOM

STILL
ROOM

WOMEN
SERVANTS
SITTING
ROOM

WASHING ROOM
AND
LAUNDRY

UN
OM

LAMP
ROOM

BRUSHING
ROOM

W.C.

ERS
OM

LOBBY

KITCHEN

KITCHEN COURT

BREW
HOUSE

RT

ROOM

SCULLERY

DUST

COAL
HOUSE

RVANTS
HALL

BAKE
HOUSE

PASTRY

PANTRY

LARDER

e whole right-hand section of the house, built around the kitchen court,
ns in the 1930s. Jane Austen's favourite room, the Library, is in the wing,

Mistress of all I survey .... I have this moment seen Mrs Driver driven up to the Kitchen Door.' She could not have observed this scene except from the north side of the house, as there was no back carriageway. Then during the same visit (Letter 95), she writes: 'I am all alone: I have five tables, eight and twenty chairs and two fires all to myself.' Even allowing for jocular exaggeration, she could only be speaking of the long library, which the family used as their normal sitting-room (as Jane confirms in Letter 89, 'We live in the Library except at meals'), and the 'two fires' are clearly shown in the 1874 plan. It was this room which Marianne Knight remembered when she described how her aunt,

> would sit quietly working [sewing] beside the fire in the library, saying nothing for a good while, and then would suddenly burst out laughing, jump up and run across the room to a table where pens and paper were lying, write something down, and then come back to the fire and go on quietly working as before.[11]

Unhappily, it is this room which was subsequently most altered and subdivided.

Upstairs, we face more of a problem. There is no first-floor plan in the 1874 brochure, but the 1853 architectural drawings at Maidstone show eight bedrooms, four each side of a central corridor. These

[11] Constance Hill, *loc.cit.* p.202.

Fig. 7   *The garden front in 1874, from the sales-brochure. The central block is almost as Jane Austen knew it, but the big service wing to the left, with the pediment, was added by her nephew Edward Knight junior after her death.*

rooms were much altered in succeeding years when the household expanded, and bathrooms, which did not exist in Regency houses, were annexed to the bedrooms. It is therefore impossible to identify Jane's 'Yellow Room' where she worked after breakfast (Letters 52 and 53), or the 'little chintz room' which she greatly admired after Edward re-decorated it (Letter 89), or Fanny Knight's 'Green room at the end of the gallery' or the 'White Room'. Chapman suggests

Fig. 8 *The entrance front today. Comparing this with the 1790 engra*

it is evident how few the changes to this front have been since then.

that the 'Hall Chamber' (Letter 52) may have been the room above the hall. Otherwise we are lost. If only Jane had written, 'I have left the door open between the Yellow Room and the Hall Chamber, and I can see the Temple from the windows', but such clues are denied us.

Edward had many servants. In 1820 there were nineteen at Chawton,[12] and that there was accommodation for many more at Godmersham is evident from the 1853 plans of the upper floors of the wings and in the attics, which may also have contained the day and night nurseries, for Jane writes (Letter 52), '[Lizzy and Charles] and their attendant have the boys' attic'. She may seldom have visited these remoter parts of the house, for there was enough bustle in the rest of it. 'In this house', she wrote to her brother Francis (Letter 90), 'there is a constant succession of small events, somebody is always going or coming.' One must imagine them ordering carriages, demanding tea, games and conversation, greeting guests, consuming enormous meals and placating harassed servants. With eleven children claiming the attention of their aunt, Godmersham must sometimes have been a nightmare to Jane Austen, but she had great patience with them and there were rooms for periodic escape where she could be alone.

---

[12] Margaret Wilson, *loc.cit.*, p.46.

Edward Knight died in 1832, aged 85, after a blameless life as a country squire. He was succeeded by his eldest son, also Edward, to whom he bequeathed the house and an estate of over 5,000 acres. For a quarter of a century Edward junior had been raising his large family in the big house at Chawton, and had no wish to uproot them.[13] But a year after his father's death, he made a surprising decision. Having no intention of living at Godmersham himself, he added enormously to its services and accommodation. To the pavilions that linked the main house to the wings he added two storeys that contained at least six new bedrooms, and west of the old servants' quarters and behind the west wing, he built a large kitchen court and more bedrooms above it for extra staff. The services then occupied as much space as the family's living quarters, as shown on the 1874 ground-plan (fig. 6). At the same time he replaced the Georgian sash-windows by Victorian plate-glass, and painted the whole outside of the house, brick and stone, a dull battleship grey. The result is shown in the drawing of the garden front in the 1874 brochure (fig. 7).

Edward then let the house to Carnegie Jervis, who succeeded his grandfather as 3rd Viscount St Vincent in 1859. In 1874 Edward put the whole estate up for sale, including its fifteen farms. It was bought for

[13] *Jane Austen's Family* by Maggie Lane (1984), p.235.

£225,000 by John Cunliffe Lister Kay, the son of a wealthy Midlands manufacturer. Kay died in 1902, and was succeeded by his brother Ellis, who was raised to the peerage as Lord Masham for his many inventions in the textile industry. His two sons in turn inherited the title and the estate, but never lived at Godmersham. In 1921 the 3rd Lord Masham sold the property to the 6th Earl of Dartmouth, who in 1933 re-sold it to Robert Tritton, the art-dealer, and his American wife Elsie, widow of Sir Bernhard Baron, chairman of the Carreras tobacco firm.

So frequent a change of owner and tenant had resulted in the slow deterioration of the house, the dispersal of its contents and the erosion of its estates. When Avray Tipping visited Godmersham in 1920, he found the family portraits in the drawing-room replaced by mirrors, and the library 'abandoned and decayed'.[14] The opposite wing, which had contained the kitchen and bakehouse, had become a squash court. Miraculously, the north (entrance) façade of 1732 remained intact, like the stuccoed hall and drawing-room.

In 1935-8 the Trittons set about restoring and embellishing the house with great imagination, gusto and expense. The plans of their architect, Walter Sorel, show that they allowed the north front to remain untouched apart from cleaning the grey paint off the

[14] *Country Life*, November 6, 1920.

Fig. 9   *The portico of the south front, added in the 1780s, was removed to the garden in the 1930s.*

brickwork and restoring the Georgian windows, but they demolished all the Victorian service buildings, and rebuilt them more conveniently on the east side, where they were accessible from the public road. Surprisingly, they did not restore the long library, but divided it into three bedrooms for menservants and a servants' hall.

Fig.10 *The garden front today. This was substantially altered in the 19th*

...ries, and Jane Austen would not have recognised it as the house she knew.

Their main alterations were to the south front and the rooms behind it. Sorel took down the whole of the outside wall, removed the baywindows and the Ionic porch (which he rebuilt as a garden temple facing the front), constructed a graceful orangery where the long service-wing had been, and rebuilt this side of the house using the unpainted surfaces of the original bricks to create a long neo-Georgian façade of great beauty. He had turned a grimace into a smile. The garden, too, was remodelled by Norah Lindsay as three walled courtyards, with swimming-pool and tennis-court attached.

Inside the house, the Trittons moved the main staircase to the west wing, and by adjusting the walls of the hallway where it had been, made a saloon overlooking their new terrace and lawn. They moved the dining-room to what had been the 'south' drawing room, and made a library out of the previous study, expanding each of these rooms outwards when the wall was rebuilt and the bays and portico removed. They totally reorganised the first floor and attics, making ten major bedrooms and nine smaller ones, with bathrooms to match. Jane Austen's Yellow Room, wherever it had been, was swallowed up in the reconstruction.

The Trittons filled these rooms with fine antique furniture mainly of Jane Austen's period, and brought in from London, Bath and elsewhere original fittings like fireplaces and door-cases to match those found *in situ*. When Christopher Hussey visited Godmersham in 1945 for *Country Life*, he found it a lovely reincarnation of the house that the Knights had enjoyed before the Victorians tampered with it. Jane Austen would have failed to recognise the garden front, but she would have been totally familiar with the view she had so often enjoyed as she approached the house across the park.

Robert Tritton died in 1957 and his widow in 1983. After her death there was a famous auction of the contents which raised a total of £4 million. The estate was bought by the Sunley family. They undertook a major programme of repair, and in 1992 let the house to the Infocheck Group, the worldwide business and financial information specialists, for their administrative headquarters. They have treated the house with great delicacy, leaving the hall open and main ground floor rooms free for conferences and other meetings. Both Infocheck Equifax Europe and the Sunley family are very conscious of Godmersham's long history and its associations with Jane Austen, allowing interested groups to visit the house by prior arrangement and to use it for social occasions.

Acknowledgements

The photographs were taken by Ian Pooley of Tenterden, Kent, apart from the portrait of Jane Austen by her sister (National Portrait Gallery), and of her brother Edward, and sister-in-law Elizabeth (née Bridges) after the miniature by Richard Cosway (Jane Austen Memorial Trust).

Book List

Jane Austen: a biography	Elizabeth Jenkins
A Portrait of Jane Austen	David Cecil
The World of Jane Austen	Nigel Nicolson
Jane Austen's Letters, 3rd edn,	ed. Deirdre Le Faye
Jane Austen in Kent	David Waldron Smithers
Almost another sister: the family life of Fanny Knight	Margaret Wilson
Jane Austen's England	Maggie Lane

THE JANE AUSTEN SOCIETY was founded in 1940 with the purpose of raising funds to preserve the cottage in the village of Chawton, Hampshire, where Jane Austen lived with her mother and sister from 1809 until her death in 1817. There she revised her three early novels for publication and wrote the three novels of her maturity – *Mansfield Park, Emma* and *Persuasion*.

The Society aims to foster the appreciation and study of the life, work and times of Jane Austen and the Austen family; to support the work of the Jane Austen Memorial Trust in maintaining the Museum at Chawton; and to continue a programme of scholarly publications concerning Jane Austen.

Enquiries to the Hon. Secretary:

> Mrs McCartan
> Carton House
> Medstead, Alton
> Hampshire GU34 5PE